School Lunch

by Glen Franklin and Sue Bodman
illustrated by Mélanie Florian

'Can I have some rice, please?'

3

'Can I have some chicken, please?'

'Can I have some salad, please?'

'Can I have some fruit, please?'

'Can I have some milk, please?'

'Oh no!'

'Can I have some more, please?'

School Lunch Glen Franklin and Sue Bodman

Teaching notes written by Sue Bodman and Glen Franklin

Using this book

Developing reading comprehension

A child requests his lunch. But as he walks to his table, the milk spills. He has to ask for another drink. A question structure is repeated on each page with a change in noun.

Grammar and sentence structure

- Text is well-spaced to support the development of one-to-one correspondence.

- The position of the text on each page is clear and supportive of understanding to read the left page before the right.

- 'Please' is located on a new line, supporting the phrasing of a question.

Word meaning and spelling

- Check vocabulary predictions by looking at the first letter ('rice', 'chicken', 'salad', 'fruit', 'milk').

- Using a simple repeated question structure.

- Reinforce recognition of frequently occurring words *Can, I, have, some*.

Curriculum links

Science – A blind food tasting activity will encourage language to describe taste and temperature; warm/cold; sweet/sour; hard/soft.

Geography – What is on offer for lunch at school today? How does this compare with other children in another part of the world?

Learning Outcomes

Children can:

- understand that print carries meaning and is read from left to right, top to bottom

- read some high-frequency words

- show an understanding of the sequence of events.

A guided reading lesson

Introducing the text

Give each pupil a copy of the book and read the title.

Orientation

Give a brief orientation to the text: *This boy is putting his school lunch onto his tray. Let's hope he carries it carefully.*

Preparation

Pages 2 and 3: *He's asking for some rice. He says 'Can I have some rice, please?'* Demonstrate tracking along the text as you read. Then ask the children to practise saying the question a few times, before asking them to track the print.

Pages 4 and 5: *What do you think he is asking for now? Check the picture. Yes, chicken. Let's see if we can find the word 'chicken' by reading along the sentence.* As a group, track the sentence word by word until you reach the word *'chicken'*. Then say: *Here it is. This word says chicken.* Then ask the children to read the complete sentence themselves, tracking carefully as they do.

Pages 6 and 7: *Now he asks for some 'salad'. Let's find the word 'salad'.* Again, track word by word until you reach the word *'salad'*. Ask the children to leave their finger under the word *'salad'* and ask; *How do we know this is the one that says 'salad'? Yes, it has 's' as the first letter. We know to get our mouths ready to say /s/.* Then ask the children to read the complete sentence themselves, tracking carefully as they do.

Pages 6-9: Ask the children to find the word that has changed by looking carefully at the first letter. Reinforce checking the first letter information and the illustration to confirm the noun.

Pages 10 and 11: Ask the children to look at the picture and report what has happened in